An Airplane's Day

by Harriet Loy
Illustrated by Mike Byrne

BELLWETHER MEDIA
MINNEAPOLIS, MN

Blastoff! Missions takes you on a learning adventure! Colorful illustrations and exciting narratives highlight cool facts about our world and beyond. Read the mission goals and follow the narrative to gain knowledge, build reading skills, and have fun!

Traditional Nonfiction

Narrative Nonfiction

Blastoff! Universe

MISSION GOALS

> FIND YOUR SIGHT WORDS IN THE BOOK.

> LEARN ABOUT HOW AIRPLANES GET READY TO FLY.

> THINK ABOUT QUESTIONS TO ASK WHILE YOU READ.

This edition first published in 2023 by Bellwether Media, Inc.

No part of this publication may be reproduced in whole or in part without written permission of the publisher. For information regarding permission, write to Bellwether Media, Inc., Attention: Permissions Department, 6012 Blue Circle Drive, Minnetonka, MN 55343.

Library of Congress Cataloging-in-Publication Data

LC record for An Airplane's Day available at: https://lccn.loc.gov/2022013624

Text copyright © 2023 by Bellwether Media, Inc. BLASTOFF! MISSIONS and associated logos are trademarks and/or registered trademarks of Bellwether Media, Inc.

Editor: Christina Leaf   Designer: Andrea Schneider

Printed in the United States of America, North Mankato, MN.

This is **Blastoff Jimmy**! He is here to help you on your mission and share fun facts along the way!

Table of Contents

A Busy Day.......................4

Ready to Fly!....................8

Into the Air.....................14

Ready to Land...................18

Glossary........................22

To Learn More..................23

Beyond the Mission...........24

Index...........................24

A Busy Day

The sun rises over the airport. The **hangar** doors open. The airplane comes out to greet the day. Good morning!

hangar

The airplane has a busy day ahead. It needs to move people and **cargo** to another city.

It moves to a **gate** to get ready to fly.

gate

crew

Pilots and crew check the airplane. They make sure it is safe to fly.

fuel truck

A **fuel truck** drives up to the airplane. Workers hook up a hose and add fuel.

People **board** the airplane and find their seats. They are excited for their trip!

Suitcases and other cargo are loaded below.

pilot

suitcases

Everyone is on board!
The crew closes
the airplane's doors.

runway

The airplane backs away from the gate and **taxis** to the **runway**.

The airplane waits
for its turn to take off.
It boosts its **engines**
to full power and races
down the runway.
It lifts into the air!

engines

14

JIMMY SAYS

Most planes lift off the ground at more than 150 miles (241 kilometers) per hour!

The airplane's **landing gear** closes. The airplane flies high into the sky. Inside, people begin to move around. The crew passes out snacks.

Ready to Land

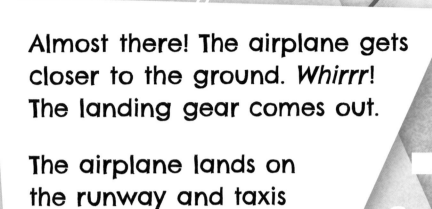

Almost there! The airplane gets closer to the ground. *Whirrr*! The landing gear comes out.

The airplane lands on the runway and taxis to the gate.

landing gear

People exit the airplane.
Below, the cargo is unloaded.

Other people wait to board.
The airplane must get ready
for its next flight!

Airplane Jobs

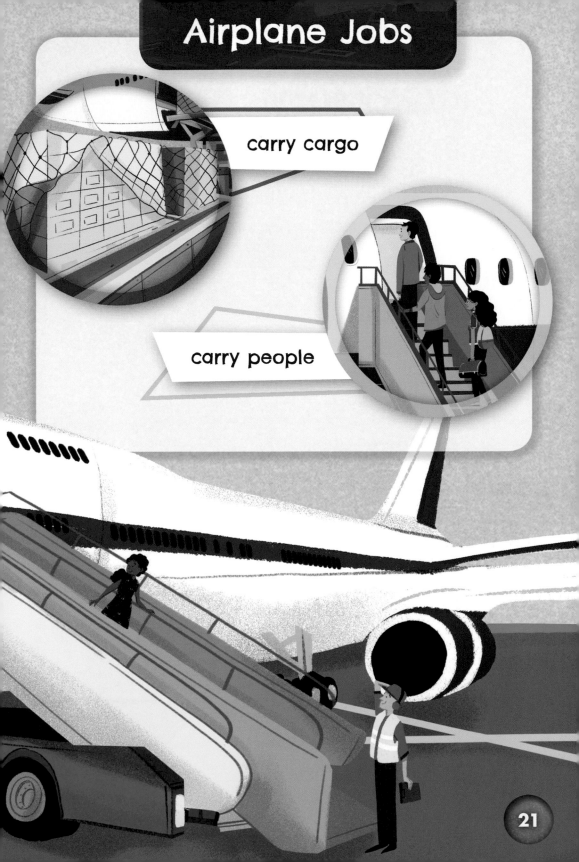

carry cargo

carry people

Glossary

board–to get on

cargo–goods carried on an airplane; mail, food, medicine, and vehicles are all kinds of cargo.

engines–the parts of an airplane that make it go

fuel truck–a truck that carries fuel; fuel trucks pump fuel into airplanes and other machines.

gate–the part of an airport where a plane parks so people can get on board

hangar–a large building where airplanes are kept

landing gear–wheels on an airplane that go in and out of the plane; landing gear lets a plane take off and land.

runway–a long, smooth surface where airplanes take off and land

taxis–moves slowly on the ground

To Learn More

AT THE LIBRARY

Duling, Kaitlyn. *Airplanes*. Minneapolis, Minn.: Bellwether Media, 2022.

Gifford, Clive. *How Airports Work*. Oakland, Calif.: Lonely Planet Kids, 2018.

Meister, Cari. *Airplanes*. North Mankato, Minn.: Pebble, 2019.

ON THE WEB

FACTSURFER

Factsurfer.com gives you a safe, fun way to find more information.

1. Go to www.factsurfer.com.

2. Enter "airplanes" into the search box and click 🔍.

3. Select your book cover to see a list of related content.

BEYOND THE MISSION

> WHERE WOULD YOU LIKE TO FLY ON AN AIRPLANE?

> DRAW A PICTURE OF WHAT YOU THINK AN AIRPLANE FROM THE FUTURE WOULD LOOK LIKE.

> WHAT IS SOMETHING FROM THE BOOK THAT SURPRISED YOU?

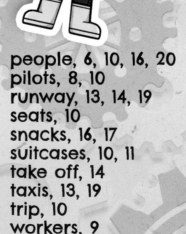

Index

airport, 4
board, 10, 12, 20
cargo, 6, 10, 11, 20
city, 6
crew, 8, 12, 16
engines, 14
fly, 6, 8, 16
fuel truck, 9
gate, 6, 7, 13, 19
hangar, 4, 5
jobs, 21
landing gear, 16, 19
lands, 19
lifts, 14, 15

people, 6, 10, 16, 20
pilots, 8, 10
runway, 13, 14, 19
seats, 10
snacks, 16, 17
suitcases, 10, 11
take off, 14
taxis, 13, 19
trip, 10
workers, 9